The Life Of The Homeless

There are too many people who are going homeless. They may have lost everything. They know how they want to live.

Sandy Smith

TABLE OF CONTENTS

building

Chapter 1

Marie drove past this huge building, bigger than a Wal-Mart store. The building had a For Sale sign. Marie saw a car there and thought she would check it out to see if the realtor was there. The realtor was there as she thought it was in her mind. The realtor asked Marie if she would like to see the place. Marie said, "Yes, please."

As the realtor showed Marie around, Marie thought to herself, "Good thing I brought my dad with me." Marie's dad was in the realtor business himself and he knew what to look for. Marie had a dream of opening a homeless shelter. Marie was thrilled with what she had seen and asked a lot of questions, knowing that you should ask questions when looking at an empty store and houses.

At the end Marie asked how much the building was. Marie said that she had to talk it over with her dad in her car.

As Marie and her dad talked about it, Marie's dad told her what he thought. Marie's dad told her that he didn't see anything wrong with the building and the price was good. Marie's dad told her that it's a choice that she has to make on her own. Marie went ahead and made the choice to buy the building. Marie told the realtor that she wants to buy the place. The realtor and Marie went over the contract and Marie handed the realtor the money.

Marie had thought on what she wanted to do with it. One side was for the homeless people to come in. The back is going to be the kitchen and off to the side will be a dining room. There was already a place for the bathroom and it was huge. A bathroom for the men and a bathroom for the women. There were ten stalls and ten showers. A spot for a store. Marie hadn't decided what to do with it at the moment.

Marie had thought about getting a decorator to come in from the TV network to see what they think. Marie thought that it was a good idea to get their help. The way the decorator thought to themselves on how to make it work for the building. Marie even mentioned adding on additional rooms to the building if necessary and Marie listened to them to see what they come up with.

Once the decorator came up with a solution, Marie went with what they had to say. They gave Marie three choices and only one that Marie had to go with. Marie went with option two, since Marie wanted the place to be a lot bigger to put the homeless people at.

CHAPTER 2

Marie had someone in mind for the store. The store is called Helping Hand Store. A store that anyone can come in and find items for their house and other things.

There were people who brought in items that they no longer needed for whatever reason. The gal paid Marie $600 a month. The gal recycled her cans, bottles and glass jars for extra money. The gal's one customer seen her loading her truck and wasn't for sure what it was. The customer asked her what she was loading onto her truck. She mentioned to the customer that they are glass jars. That she had 15 more boxes to get after having 15 boxes in her truck. The customer says, "I'll give you $350 for all of the jars." The gal was all for it and told the customer "Thank You." The customer loaded the glass jars into the U-Haul that the customer was in that she was using from a friend. The gal's name is Ashley.

A lady comes into the store and found clothes for herself

and her two children along with kitchen items for an affordable price. The young lady had asked Ashley what to do with her two twin daughters of the age of ten. Ashley had a great idea and the young lady looked around and found glass jars, tinsels, and ribbon. The young lady paid only a little bit, then spent the weekend with her girls getting the items ready to give as a gift for Christmas to the homeless. How sweet, the mother thought.

The mother and the twin girls thought that they'll start collecting their glass jars that they used from the store (doesn't matter as long they are pickle jars, spaghetti jars, and whatever glass jars that there is). The gal and the girls decided to come up with their own ideas. Once they collected a lot of jars that they'll see what they'll have to decorate the jars.

As they gather their craft stuff that they'll bring in the glass jars into their craftroom, they started in on their ideas on what they had in mind. The twins thought that they ought to have a yard sale along with their mom in their front yard to see how many people would buy.

They set their tables up and added their items up along with their unused things that the twin girls don't play with and other stuff. What doesn't sell, the mother would take to Helping Hand Store where she found the stuff for her, her girls, and their place. The mother and the girls decided to have their own table and the items that sell will go to that person (to the mother and to the twin girls).

At the end of the sale, the mother brought in close to $2,000. The oldest girl brought in close to $2,500 and the youngest girl brought in close to $2,999. The mother and the girls thought it was amazing on how their crafts went fast at first. The crafts went fast for the first 6 hours. At the last 2½ hours it was slow but the stuff that they had left went. All the items sold that first day.

The second day as they gathered all their crafts together, they put that money together. The second day of their sale was useful for them. They put the money together and raised $15,000. They took that money and got food in the house. The bills were already paid for the month from the girl's dad.

CHAPTER 3

It has been twenty years since Marie owned the homeless shelter. This young lady of the age of twenty-six years old went there to see Marie. As the gal went to talk to Marie, Marie didn't know who the young lady was until the young lady told Marie. The young lady told Marie that she took her, her two sisters and three brothers, and their mom in from the cold weather. Marie helped the young lady's mom to get from drugs and the beer that her ex-boyfriend got the mother hooked on.

Marie asked the young lady what brought her to Marie. The young lady told Marie, "Thank you for everything you done for me, my sisters, my brothers, and my mom." Marie told her that she's welcome. Marie asked about where they were. The young lady said that the kids are in school and that she is taking care of them herself. Marie asked what happened to her mom. The young lady told Marie that her mom was killed by a drunk driver. Marie says, "I am sorry to hear that." The young lady said, "Thank you."

Marie took the young lady into her office. Marie asked

the young lady on what she's doing to support herself and the young children. The young lady told Marie that she's working at Hillshire Farm, which pays $9.00 an hour. That the young lady doesn't know how much longer that she'll be there.

Knowing that the young lady is busy with her brothers and sisters, Marie suggested that she'll help the young lady to get into a job that pays $15.00 an hour. Marie also asked the young lady where she and her siblings are living at. The young lady told her where she was living at. When Marie heard where she and her siblings were staying at. That the young lady wasn't paying anything. Marie got her U-Haul and got the young lady and her sibling's stuff that Marie put the young lady into a place near the homeless place so the young lady's siblings could stay in the school district and that Marie could help the young lady out in any way that she could.

Marie contacted the company that pays $15.00 an hour and the young lady got in and started the job. The young lady didn't know what to expect. The young lady "LOVED" the job. The young lady saved up enough money. The young lady turned to Marie and got her help on buying a home for her and her siblings. The young lady wanted to get into an 6 bedroom home where she could afford it. Marie knew her stuff after her dad told her what to look for. The young lady was thankful that she got Marie's help. The young lady got settled into her home with her siblings under the age of 15 years old. Everyone is happy and much more.

CHAPTER 4

When Marie receives a call from the Sheriff letting her know about bringing these people in to her shelter, Marie never turns people away. Marie is one of those people who has the care in the world. Marie tends to help others out in any way possible.

Marie had helped tons of people by helping the person find a job and find a place to live. She helped people rebuild their house, help them find a day care, help them find a school, and whatever the case maybe. The people who were there at Marie's shelter gave her money to help her out when they were there.

One day Marie thought to herself, she has this huge lot. She thought that she should have another shelter like she has now, but one to keep the children away from the men that mothers don't want their young children to be around.

The following day that Marie went to the City Hall and see about another homeless shelter. Marie was approved, and the following week, the contractors started on the building the place. Once it was all done, Marie was thrilled to have it done. Marie had more than enough to keep everyone happy.

Marie used that building to put single mothers into that shelter to keep the single mothers and their children safe from the other people. Marie is pleased to see things going as smooth as she pleased. Marie's dad was happy to see the shelter going great. Everyone "LOVES" Marie.

HELP THE HOMELESS

CHAPTER 5

Billie Jo Anderson and Todd Painting lost their home. Billie's place was flooded and she had to leave her home. Billie Jo Anderson had no place to go. Billie stayed in the back of a van, in tents, and wherever Billie could sleep.

Todd's place caught on fire. Todd wasn't happy that he lost his home that he'd had for 29 years. Todd slept at the riverbanks, in tents, in the back of vehicles, and anywhere Todd could sleep.

One day Billie Jo and Todd seen each other for the first time in 28 to 30 years. Billie Jo and Todd gave each other a huge hug. They couldn't believe they hadn't seen each other for so long. Billie Jo and Todd spoke for hours. Todd looked at the time and thought he better get somewhere safe. Billie asked Todd if there's a shelter near by. Todd said yes and that it was 6 to 8 blocks from where they were. Billie wanted to take a shower and get into fresh clothes.

Billie and Todd got to the shelter. Marie asked how she could help them. Billie and Todd mentioned to Marie that they wanted a shower and clean clothes along with a good night sleep. Marie helped them. Billie and Todd were glad to be there.

After cleaning up, Billie Jo and Todd went to the front room of the shelter to sit down, and they talked for two to three more hours until they seen the time. They went to their rooms and turned in to bed. Billie Jo and Todd thought to themselves, Would there be a chance for them to be a couple after all they went through in losing their homes?

The following day as they were getting around, Billie Jo and Todd met in the kitchen to get a bit to eat and drink. Todd asked Billie Jo if she is seeing anyone or married. Billie Joe told Todd that her husband passed away 6 years ago. He had a stroke and it killed him. Billie Jo has 4 kids and they are in their 20s. Billie Jo mentioned to Todd that after her husband passed away that she has been busy taken care of her kids. Todd said to Billie Jo that he was sorry for her loss. That Billie Jo hadn't thought about dating since her husband past. Billie Jo felt something there between her and Todd. That spark between Todd and Billie Jo was back.

Todd asked Billie Jo if she would give him another chance. Billie Jo thought about it for a few moments and said yes to Todd. They were both happy. Todd felt like he was on the moon once again.

Billie Jo asked Todd if he was married and had kids.

Todd told Billie that he was married and that his wife had passed away 5 years ago. Todd has two twin boys who are 25, and that they have twin girls that are 20 years old. Billie Jo said that she was sorry to hear about his loss.

As Billie Jo and Todd spent their days together, they found a place in another town. They didn't want to live in Savannah, Missouri. There were too many memories there for Billie Jo. They found a cute place in Gower, Missouri. After being together for 4 years, Todd asked Billie Jo to marry him. Billie Jo said yes. Todd and Billie were happy. Todd's kids liked Billie Joe and her kids liked Todd. Billie, Todd and their kids were all happy.

CHAPTER 6

Amy and Alex got to thinking to themselves on how they could help the homeless. Amy thought about quilting and knitting. Alex thought about jewelry, hand bags, and crafting. Basically, Amy and Alex came up with the same things to help the homeless. Amy and Alex made a profit of $2,975 and went to Marie's shelter and gave her the money to support the homeless. Marie told them that they didn't have to do it. Amy and Alex said that they wanted to do it. Marie didn't argue with them and accepted the donation.

You would be surprised what people can do to help others when they see homeless people. Amy and Alex enjoy doing the things that they do. The things that Amy and Alex does for a living makes them happy. It tends to keep them busy.

CHAPTER 7

Since Marie opened the shelter 20 years ago, Marie and the volunteers teaches people job skills. When the people gets a place of their own, and they get a steady job and learn the job, they are blessed. Marie and her staff tends to teach the people there at the shelter to help them organize birthday parties for the kids that the kids would never forget. The party for the kids was a hit at the shelter. The presents and the cake the kids enjoy.

One day a young girl came to Marie and the staff. The young girl told them, "Thank you for allowing my parents have a party here at the shelter," The young girl said to them. That was a party that she never forgot. Knowing that they cared.

CHAPTER 8

There have been people who came up to Marie and asked her about opening an restaurant. Marie said that's a good idea. That Marie wondered what to do with that building that was six blocks from where her shelter is. Marie's friend who she'd known all her life knew of someone who could repair the problems to that restaurant.

The friend's cousin, Don, was there with his crew. The cousin was outside smoking a cigarette. She mentioned to her cousin about Marie. Marie told him what she was looking for having done. He said that he wanted to look at the building.

They met over there at the restaurant. Once Marie showed him around, she asked him how much it would cost her to have it fixed. He told Marie, and Marie said okay, the job is his. He took the job that day with his crew. It only took him and his crew 45 days to do the job.

The last day Don called Marie over. As Marie stepped into the place, Marie was blown away. Marie loved the way Don thought and the way Marie described her thought to him. All Marie said that it was beautiful. All Marie has to do is put her touch on it.

Once it was ready to open, Marie thought of a gal who enjoyed cooking and baking. The person that Marie had in mind is Sandi. Marie called her and explained to Sandi what she wanted. Sandi took the job. Marie was thrilled. Sandi got a small crew to work with her.

Sandi thought to herself that she'd give Marie rent that Marie wants monthly and whatever extra that Sandi brought in. Everyone LOVED Sandi's cooking. People tended to put in a tip for Sandi. There were tip jars with a lock for each employee. Marie thought that was smart. Sandi and her co-workers tends to make sweets. The thing is, Sandi had a printout asking everyone to put their favorite dish down that they tried that they liked. The customers did. Half of the money would go to help Marie with the homeless.

CHAPTER 9

Marie thought to herself one day, with all of the changes that Marie had made in people's lives, that Marie had made an impact in people's lives.

The city came to Marie's shelter and Marie wasn't expecting it. The city handed Marie a plaque for everything Marie has done for the homeless. The city handed Marie a check of $10,000 to help out on the supplies that Marie needed for the shelter.

Helping the homeless people takes time and patience. Things can't be done when we want them to be done as we want them to be. It does take time to research things. Sometimes the answers comes to us quickly and some times they don't. The best way to find the answers is going to the website www.google.com and the answers are there.

There are times that a person would tell you information. The information from others tends to help. When you tend to forget things – that's when it jogs your memory on things.

Marie had been asked why she opened the shelter like she did. Marie's response is this. That "GOD" called me into helping the homeless people and other people in need. I enjoy helping other people. I hate seeing homeless people living on the streets. This way they have a place to stay and they aren't in the hot or cold weather.

Marie is the type of gal who is down to earth, caring, loving, and honest type person. Marie is the type of gal is very blunt about things. Marie tells it the way it is.

There are people who tends to stand behind Marie. Marie tends to help when others need the help.

When Marie opened the shelter and the restaurant it became a successful business. Marie one day surprised Sandi unexpectedly. Marie mentioned to Sandi with everything that Sandi had done for Marie and the homeless, that Marie thought that she would give Sandi supplies that she needed for the restaurant. Sandi wasn't expecting it. It took Sandi by surprise.

CHAPTER 10

There are homeless people through the United States. They tend to sleep anywhere they have to sleep. The homeless people may ask for money for food and a drink. That way they can eat and have something to drink. People may or may not give money to the homeless people. Homeless people out there stand out at a corner street or wherever to get a ride.

A lot of us tend to have our fear that they may hurt us for a lot of reasons. Granted, we have to watch for the homeless people. There are homeless people who are down to earth people.

We never know when we could go homeless. Never know that our place caught on fire or got flooded. Homeless people don't ask for much help. Let's give the homeless people a break. We may not like their life style. They do much better once they have a home.

In most states that people tends to make jewelry to help the homeless people or people may tend to do other things to help the homeless people.

What would we like to see? A better community. For everyone to come together to help others. To understand how homeless have lived on the streets. There are people in this world who are homeless. Knowing that we tend to live a normal life and doing our daily things every day. The homeless people tend to live their life like us regular people, as long as you were homeless and got the help that you got from the shelter. Knowing that, you feel better about yourself.

As long that you know of anyone who is homeless, be a part of their lives by calling him or her to see how they are. Anything that would help him or her and make a better life for him or her, knowing that he or she and or a couple (even couples with children) is going through a dreadful time. Once they get back on their feet, he or she would make sure to pay you back in any way.

CHAPTER 11

There are homeless people out and about. They wonder on how they survive. The homeless people tend to pick up cans wherever they see a can. They tend to find money on the ground. Anything to help them get through day by day.

Sometimes, the homeless tend to sell their belongings so they can get by, no matter where they are. He or she tends to ask people on the streets if they'll be interested on buying what he or she is selling. That way he or she can eat. That's the only way that they can survive day by day.

When homeless people has no money, what do they eat? Do they go searching in dumpsters to search for food? In Saint Joseph, Missouri, that there's an Open Door Food Kitchen that will give them a free meal. What would they do if there wasn't an Open Food Kitchen?

Homeless people may have to search for food. Sometimes homeless people tends to go without food. A person would be surprised what a homeless person can do when it comes to food. Whatever he or she finds, they'll make it. Other than that, as long he or she has the money, they'll go to Hardee's, Taco John's, Taco Bell, McDonald's, or Burger King to find something cheap from the dollar menu with a drink or whatever money they could afford. They can be smart when it comes to their money. You would be surprised on what they can do.

Where do homeless people live? The homeless tend to go anywhere they can find a place to sleep. There are some that will stay in shelters and some won't stay in shelters. There are some people who would sleep by the riverside. Anywhere that they can lay their bodies at night to rest.

CHAPTER 12

Most homeless has a lot of good sprits, faith, and more. They have bad and good days. All they have are their friends at the shelter. The homeless people may consider the employees as friends, though it all depends on the person. They are the closest people that they have as family or friends. They are close as any one can be. Plus they tend to have each other's back when they are in public and or where they'll be.

Most homeless struggle with the bullying, teasing. They get beaten up on, raped, and they're around people who are addicted to alcohol and drugs. Those who lives on the streets some times faces social requirement. They are labeled as lazy, knowing that they're not. Most of them had served our country.

They feel bad that they lost what they had.

They've lost their spouse, their kids and their family. Sometimes the sisters, brothers, parents, and the rest of the family wants nothing to do with him or her.

They've lost their job. Or they're mentally ill, abusers, or criminals. They aren't any different and they don't want to be treated any different.

Respect is always earned. There are homeless people who want to make a difference in their lives. They want to get clean by stop drinking and to get off the drugs. They tend to find the source to get the help he or she needs. He or she wants to make a better life. They don't like the way they're living. They go to a shelter to get help. A shelter would help him or her on the right path. He or she knows that they can do it as long they set their minds to doing it. When they are thankful that they received.

To those of you who wants to change your life around. Only you can make that choice. You have to make the decision to be a better you. Set yourself a goal.

1. To get off drugs
2. To stop drinking

3. To get what you need

4. To help myself is to be a better me by helping myself before helping others

5. To prove to others that I can do it.

It's amazing how people got the help.

They aren't homeless anymore. They got the help that they needed. They don't drink and do drugs like they used to. They are working. They are a lot happier.

We tend to wonder if the homeless people have emotions like a lot of us do. The answer to that is "YES." They tend to struggle with their own emotions. He or she has these thoughts in their head. Why does things have to happen to me? Why did my place burn or flood? Why am I doing the things that I'm doing?

Whatever the reason may be on the "WHY," the

homeless struggle like everybody else does. Most of the homeless are thankful that they are getting the help that they are. They are thankful for the things that they've done while they were staying in the shelter, when they got their life straightened out.

Five to ten years down the road, he or she and or the couple tends to help the homeless people with what they had learned when they were homeless. They struggle with the things that they had dealt with. The thoughts about what their parents and other relatives may have said to him or her will stay with them forever.

CHAPTER 13

8th Street Community is in Saint Joseph, Missouri. They tend to help folks in need. They are trying to engage other churches, social service agencies, and the surrounding area to come together as a community to tackle the tough issues in our surrounding area when it comes to the homeless and the people who served our country. They have help for drug addition, hunger, and they have programs for the offenders. The Crossing Ministry has a drop-in center. They do basic need. There's a clothes closet, washer and dryer facilities, showers are available, along with case workers who will assist in housing need and much more. They have a worship center. They are open daily to those in need. They have things to do for those who want to work to earn various products in their company store, share in the sales of crafts, and or whatever it may be. They have a greenhouse on site. So many things that people can learn in a day-to-day life.

28

CHAPTER 14

When you live in a town that has buses to get you from point A to point B, it's not always enough to get you where you need to go. Even though Kansas City, Missouri, has a bus system to get you around. There should be better transportation. The other towns such as Savannah, Rosendale, Fillmore, Cosby, and the surrounding areas ought to think of those who has to walk to the store, bank, or wherever he or she has to go. Andrew County and other parts of Missouri ought to think of having an bus system like Saint Joseph and Kansas City has. That way, adults and children can get where they need to go instead of relying on people, such as their friends and family.

Missouri ought to have a better bus system. Saint Joseph has the Saint Joseph Transit, Oats Bus, and taxi cabs. There are people who can't afford to pay for an taxi cab. Oats Bus costs $2.00 to $3.00 to get to the doctor appointments. Saint Joseph Transit for an disability is .50 cents and for non-disability is a $1.00. For drop off to an destination is $1.00.

There should be places here in Missouri where people

can come together and make a better and safer place. The homeless don't want to feel scared, hopeless, and worthless. They want to be a better person.

WAKE UP MISSOURI: What could we do to have more transportation for those who need it?

CHAPTER 15

There should be Day Labor in the Saint Joseph and Savannah areas. There's not a lot of jobs in those towns. They ought to have more jobs. Plus the minimum wages for the low income people needs to be high enough to pay the bills.

Some people don't want to work without having a good reason. They don't want to make a minimum wage as most people and or low-class people. Most of them don't know how to budget their money, like buying things that they want instead of what they need. [Example: beer, drugs, and other unwanted items.] They don't know how to live without those items and focus on the items that they need.

For those who are interested in working, Day Labor for them is like working daily (full or part time jobs) and getting paid weekly, every two weeks, or monthly. It's great for those people. They are in the community making something for him or her. It's always good to have an daytime job stead of working the night shift. There are jobs that pays over $10.00 an hour and that they can afford high-dollar items.

The jobs that pays $7.00 to $9.00 an hour has to watch their money. Especially when they pay rent or mortgage, bills, household items, things for their kids and their pets, and meds. There's only $5.00 or less. How is anyone supposed to live? There should be better paying jobs.

There are some people who don't work because they have health issues or special needs. When they go through United Cerebral Palsy and certain places to get work skills, they see what he or she is good at and then place them at certain places to work. One is called Specialty Industries. Most of them have some special needs. The ones who works at Specialty Industries tends to get made fun of. The way he or she dresses. Whatever the deal maybe. A few may have some sort of mental issues and some may not. Those who has a special needs tends to get made fun off along with the homeless. All the special needs and the homeless people wants is for people to stop making front of them, stop teasing them, and much more. They want to work like a normal people does. They want to be treated as you and everyone does.

Let's treat the special people and the homeless as they want to be treated. When it comes to homeless people, they don't want to be labeled as homeless. There's not a number on the homeless population. Most homeless people want to work, to get paid under the table, to get paid so they can get their medicines. Most homeless people tends to work for three days. Most homeless tends to stay at the job so they can make a better person of themselves. Most homeless people tends to expect a free hand out. That's not how it works these days. As long that they want something. That they have to work for it instead of getting it for free.

Let's Build More Companies That Pays Good And Help Others.

You would be surprised what a homeless person can do with their hands. Whatever he or she finds on the streets and the items that they can do. The item can be glass item, aluminum item, or any item that you can imagine. We all (homeless or not) that they like good game plain to make something out of the item. Every person is very creative in his or her way (as long that they set their minds to it on being creative). A homeless person has ability in their own way. A way the person's mind works on making things. Being creative is art to a lot of people.

When an homeless person makes something that he or she draws it on paper as they see it in their head. Once the project is done that he or she will try their best to sell the item. Most homeless people would ask if there's an particular piece that you are looking for and they'll let you know if they have it or not. Most likely that he or she may have it or it may catch your eye on the item. Others tends to like what the homeless makes.

We got to give the homeless credit for what they do. Never give him or her a bad rap for trying their hardest to make something out of themselves. He or she bust themselves to be creative. The homeless person wants to make an difference. Never know what type of additions that he or she would add to their stuff.

CHAPTER 16

Living in a school bus isn't a place that we were expecting to be in. It's better than laying on the streets or wherever we have to sleep at. Larry G. Smith lived in a bus on a couple's property in Bolckow, Missouri. Some people thought that Larry was crazy to be living in a bus. Only Larry had to do what was best for him since Larry had no other option to live. Living in a bus is better than living on the streets, or in abandoned homes and businesses, because those places can get you into trouble with the law.

Larry's youngest daughter didn't know that Larry lived in a school bus till years later when Larry, Larry's girlfriend Annabell, and Larry's youngest daughter, went there to get some stuff. Larry's youngest daughter couldn't believe the way he lived. Sandy wondered how her dad ate, bathed, and had his own privacy. Sandy thought to herself on how her dad could live like this, living on a bus. There were no seats. All the seats were removed where the students would sit. Sandy doesn't remember seeing anything such as a bed, chairs, sofa, and dishes. Sandy even thought, how on earth is her dad making meals for himself. All these questions that kept coming into Sandy's head on how her dad Larry does things. Sandy kept her questions to herself.

Larry knew himself that his daughter had questions and he left it alone. All that matters is that Larry is spending time with his daughter. That's what mattered to Larry and Sandy, is father and daughter time.

The thing is with Larry though. Larry had his belongings nicely stacked. Larry had an wooden burner to keep warm in the winter months. Annabell didn't want to see Larry living in that bus.

The thing with Larry when he was living in the school bus. Larry helped this guy out when he needed the help. Larry would also pick up cans and metal as Larry spotted them to make extra money from them when Larry took them to the recycling center to support himself. When Annabell came back into Larry's life, Larry was happy to see Annabell after years past. Annabell gave Larry a place to live and made each other happy. Larry is thankful to have Annabell in his life once again. Larry had more freedom there in Liberty, Missouri than Larry had in Bolckow, Missouri. Larry was able to drive where he wants to go and or walk where he wants. Knowing that there wasn't much of anything there in Bolckow, Missouri. All there is in Bolckow, Missouri is farm life, a few bars, a post office, a gas station on the 71 Highway, and bunch of houses. That's what Larry told his youngest daughter.

Even though Larry didn't mind living in the bus. That's

all Larry knew. Sandy's understanding from Annabell that she had to ask City Hall (Wherever Annabell mentioned to Sandy, knowing that Sandy couldn't remember where Annabell said where she had to ask) to find out about having Larry move in with Annabell there in Liberty, Missouri. Annabell explained the situation and that they allowed Annabell to move in Larry.

CHAPTER 17

We can't judge someone's past, knowing that we weren't there when it had happened. Stop pretending to be something that you aren't aware of on their past. It's hard for people to explain things to you and others, knowing that it'll be with him or her for the rest of their lives. Homeless or not, you wouldn't want to share your life story on what had happened to you, would you? We're trying to cope with what happened. We're trying to comprehend on what happen physically, and emotions. Some homeless people tend to get counseling to solve their problems. Even though it's hard for him or her to talk to the counselor knowing that the counselor never been there themselves.

A question that people tends to asks you is, How does it feel to be homeless?

It's not a place where anyone wants to be at in that time of need. Those homeless people want a roof over their heads and a place to call home. They don't want to be on the streets. Those people who have a place to live are the lucky ones, to have a place to stay with a roof over their heads. To those of you who have a place (A place that you bought, or a rental place) that you ought to feel the way the homeless people feels on living on the streets.

Basically what I'm saying is, Put yourself in their place and how you would feel about living on the streets? Ask yourself this question. Would I rather live in a place with a roof over my head, or would I rather live on the streets?

Most of the homeless people have to make choices in their lives. Most homeless choose to drink and or whatever they tend to do.

There are people who aren't homeless. They see these homeless people sitting on their rear ends doing nothing. All they are doing is sitting around getting high or getting drunk or both. Knowing that they don't have the money for drugs and beer.

Wake up, homeless people. Get off your rear ends, get yourself clean, and get yourself a job. Stop feeling sorry for yourself. Go find a job and make a better you. Stop beating yourself up. Turn yourself around. Stop and look at yourself the way you are or take a before (as a druggy and when you're drinking) and after you got yourself clean. That's when you'll realize what a chance you had.

There's a place in Saint Joseph, Missouri called the "Tent City." Tent City is by Missouri River. They tend to stay in tents under the bridge or the highway, knowing that it's not the safest place to be. Most of the homeless people have no place to go. The only place that he or she can go is to the tent city to stay. Where else can they really go? They can always go to a place to stay as long they set their minds to it.

I bet this raises questions on most people's minds. Let's see if this is right. These are questions for the president. Donald Trump, had you ever thought about the homeless people? What I meant by that:

1. How could you help the homeless people?

2. How can you help the people who served our country that lost everything and that their homes with their spouse and children?

3. How can you make Missouri a better place?

4. How can you help those in need with their requests that they are looking for.

5. Melissa Penrod's Question: What will be the plan to help keep everyone safe from terrorists and war?

Knowing that there's so many questions that people wants to ask you, Donald Trump. What's your response Mr. President, Donald Trump? We all would like to know. Knowing that Missouri could always use a better environment, businesses, transportation, and much more here in Missouri.

CHAPTER 18

If you have never been homeless, what's been mentioned that it's tough to describe living on the streets. Sleeping in strange places on the streets and where have you. Going through the motions and what have you. At the same time that you are beating yourself up for being in that type of situation.

It is very surreal. No one ever thinks that he or she will become homeless until it happens to him or her. Living on the streets can be emotionally and physically exhausting. When you sleep outside, you are vulnerable to just about everything. You can be mugged, shot, beat up, and whatever. You can be scared, probably more scared than any other person will ever be, by living on the streets.

When you are homeless, no matter what you are doing and or wherever you are, you can make a difference in your life or someone else's life. No matter what you are doing, you can help others out as long that they need the help. Don't be scared to step right in and help. You could always ask if you could help them out. Step in and take action and make a difference in their life. You never know that they'll take action or give you the help that you could use. You never know what you could give help on.

When you are out and about and you see a homeless person, be kind and exchange a smile and say hi. They may have an bad day and or they may be dealing with things, whatever they may be dealing with. You never know. By exchanging a smile and a hi, you could brighten their day.

Those who work in the homeless services shelters can usually spot someone fresh to the streets. It's usually not their clothes or hygiene. It's the look of fear and confusion on their face. They'll have the look on their face that they're scared. No matter what their circumstances led him or her to their homelessness – eviction, unemployment, mental illness and or domestic violence that left them homeless for the first night, knowing that it's painful. Can you imagine how it feels when a personal crisis has hit? Knowing that you no longer have accesse to money or a place to stay.

You can always volunteer at a homeless shelter to help out and change an person's life. You never know what will come your way. Volunteering can change your life around. You can even donate your unused items that you no longer need. Your unused items would be appreciated with the shelter people and the homeless people. You would be making someone's day. You can always bring help as long it's needed. Don't be shy. Get in there and show them what you got.

Wherever you live. Check out your local websites to help the homeless. You never know that there's people making jewelry, decorating jars, and or whatever there is that people are doing to help the homeless.

CHAPTER 19

As long you were homeless. How would you help the homeless? Knowing that homeless people tend to have nothing when they live on the streets. Lets say that your homeless. What would you like to see done on the streets to make them a better and safer place? What would you like to see changed?

Do you remember the first day of being homeless? What led you to that day? Would you change anything from the first day on being on the streets? Do you feel safer "on the streets" or in your prior "HOME"?

What are your dreams? Would you go get the help that you need?

CHAPTER 20

Before buying a place. Ask questions about the building. Check out the place. Make sure that nothing is wrong. Always see it's good quality and look at the flues in the building. As long that you want to, start fresh. Look at properties to see that it's big enough on what you are looking at. Save your money until you know that you have it. Always make sure to have someone with you and make sure to have a second option.

As long that you want to open that homeless shelter, make sure to put out the word about where it's located at. That way people knows where you're at. As long that you need help (need volunteers) put in an ad. Let them know how they can reach you.

CHAPTER 21

The Jones Family lived in this trailer park in Savannah, Missouri. There was a family of six, two adults and four children.

During the night, the husband woke up and smelled gas. He went to wake his wife up to get their four children out of the trailer. The family of six got out safely.

The mother was freaked out. She didn't know what to do. Her husband told her that he has a place where his wife, four kids and himself can go for the night/morning. They went there and the kids went back to sleep as the parents watched over them. The parents got an hold of the American Red Cross and they helped the Jones Family out.

The Jones Family were thankful that the Red Cross helped them out. Mrs. Jones still had nightmares that still haunts her today. Lynda was afraid that her and her children were going to die. Lynda and the four children were fine and safe.

Websites To Go To ~ To Get Help

1. http://www.aa.org/

2. http://www.socialwelfareboard.org/

3. http://www.catholiccharities-kcsj.org/